MW01153495

STEP by STEP!

HOW THE LINCOLN SCHOOL MARCHERS BLAZED A TRAIL TO JUSTICE

Joyce Clemons, Civil Rights Hero
Hillsboro, OH, 1957

my friends Carolyn and Virginia

Debbie Rigaud & Carlotta Penn

Art by Nysha Lilly

Daydreamers Press

Imagine you had to walk six hundred miles to get fair treatment at school. When I was twelve years old, I did just that!

Together with my friends and our mothers, I marched so that Black children could get an equal education.

We had a fire for fairness burning
in our hearts. It shed a light on the
path we walked toward justice.

And boy, *did we walk!*

I want everyone to know our story,
so I kept a memory book of our
marching days.

Take a look!

, 1954

VOL. 117, NO. 10

H Firm Given Contract To
truct New Webster Scho

nds
ine

00

park-
the
ed a
for
ng
Mc-
gh
is

Lincoln

washington

Zoning map

I hope your leg feels better soon Teresa
♥ Joyce

rd of Education has agree
pictured here will continue
Schools are co
here. Repair
ated Tuesday
(aff Photo)

s Last D

Studying with other students in kitchen classroom, Joyce Mari
Clemons (2nd from l.) is plaintiff in integration legal suit.

Notes:
damo

my friend
Myra
in her
favorite
dress :)

EVERYDAY
2 MILES

School Zo... ...out; Slight... ...s S...

Rezoning of the city elementary school districts was carried out on schedule, Friday morning, although some Negro groups offered token resistance to the plan.

The new plan, included in a resolution drawn up and by the Hillsboro board on last week, drew ...one lines which, of

...wou... ...cond... ...Was... ...assign... ...the c... ...Lincol... There...

...the ...rect as some ...The only

...hown was ...hool, where ...dren had bee... ...school term... ...ed 20 colored ...owed up at the W... ...building with a smaller grou... ...adults, some of them mem... ...of the recently reactivated bra... ...of the association for advanceme... ...of colored people. The group wa...

STATE CONFERENCE
OF 75 NEGRO ELEME...
...OUSLY ALL W...
...ENT OF...

My friends Carolyn and Virginia

UNFAIR SCHOOL RULES

Before we won the school fight, Black kids in our town went to Lincoln School and White kids went to Webster.

Lincoln was a run-down, drafty building with three grades crammed together in each room. Our books were old with missing pages.

Webster was a nicer, warmer building with a room for each grade and newer schoolbooks.

But Webster wouldn't accept Black students.

That was the Hillsboro School Board's rule— even though segregation was against the law.

WEBSTER ELEMENTARY

HEARTS ON FIRE

In the summer of 1954, Lincoln School was badly damaged in a fire. The school board tried to send us back to the burnt-up school building, so our mothers ignited a plan. I saw my mom in our backyard, talking to my friend Eleanor's mother, Mrs. Imogene.

Mrs. Imogene said, "Our kids deserve a safe building."

And when our moms got together for a big meeting, she announced, "According to the law of the USA, Hillsboro cannot keep Black children in separate, unequal schools!"

The plan was set: Our moms would march with us to Webster for as long as it took for the principal to let us in!

FORWARD MARCH

January, February, March, March, March.
Our group of thirty-seven kids and nineteen
mothers walked a mile to Webster
EVERY. SINGLE. SCHOOL. DAY.
For two whole years!

Sale 99¢

DESEGREGATE NOW

1 mile to school

our BIG marching group

I CANT GO TO SCHOOL BECAUSE SEGREGATION

OUR CHILDREN PLAY TOGETHER WHY CANT THEY LEARN TO GETHER

WE WANT EQUAL EDUCATION FOR OUR CHILDREN

IF YOU WERE IN OUR PLACE WOULD IT BE DIFFERENT?

We met at Mrs. Sallie's house and marched in a "**neat and orderly group, and no messing around.**"

We started up East Street, along the sidewalk. We blazed a trail past the grocery store and the church house.

We walked through the schoolyard and up to the door, where we'd get stopped by a brick wall . . . named Principal Henry.

mrs. Hackney

KITCHEN SCHOOLS

Did you think that just because Principal Henry wouldn't let us into Webster School, we got to play all day? No way!

The mothers were our marching leaders and our **teachers**! They taught lessons at their kitchen tables with some help from the Quaker teacher Mrs. Hackney.

OCTOBER

Sun	mon	tue	wed	thu	fri	sat

PRIL

300 days
× 2 miles
a day =
600 miles!

STEP BY STEP

It wasn't easy. Some mornings, the gray skies were so dreary, I wanted to run back inside. Rain clouds hung over our heads as we passed glaring townsfolk.

Still, we marched on.

We stepped over the box lines on the calendar, across the rows of dates, and down the page, until it flipped and we started from the top again.

our moms are BRAVE.

COURAGE UNDER FIRE

Hateful people tried to scare us
by burning crosses in our front
lawns and spewing wicked words.
Some of us kids felt afraid.

Other times, we were just plain tired of marching.

We wondered, "**Why do we have to march again today when we know we'll be turned away?**"

But then I reminded my friends what Mrs. Imogene said:

" According to the law of the USA, Hillsboro cannot keep Black children in separate, unequal schools!"

Our mothers took firm footsteps forward. They declared, "**You can burn the cross to try to scare us, but we will keep on marching.**"

The fire on that cross was no match for the light in our hearts.

our moms at the courthouse

Hearing Being Held on Sch

BEST FOOT FORWARD

The mothers called attorney Constance Baker Motley to town. We sued the school board with her help. Mrs. Motley said the judges must follow our country's rules and make our town do the right thing.

Since I was one of the oldest marchers, they chose me to speak up for the students in the lawsuit. I was SO nervous, but I was proud to use my voice to help spark change.

my mom stands up for whats right even when its Hard.

I'm so proud of my mama! Joyce

Mom didn't go to jail, and we didn't stop marching. We kept going.

A BRIGHT DAY

Then, finally, the judge decided we were right: Webster would have to let Black students enroll IMMEDIATELY.

When she got the good news, Mom smiled bright like the noonday sun!

VICTORY MARCH

On our first school day as Webster students, we met at Mrs. Sallie's house with hearts on fire, and we set out on our usual path. But instead of being turned away at the school door, brick-wall-Principal Henry let us in!

We marched past unfamiliar faces and wondering whispers. We stepped into our classrooms and took our seats, where we belonged.

There were challenges at Webster, sure. Many of the kids were kind, but others never even said hello. And sometimes teachers were unfair. But we marched through each challenge, **step by step.**

We were proud of our persistence. Daddy always said, **"Give 100%. If you can give 150%, do that."** And so we did.

Integration of Colored Pupils In Elementary Schools Is Asked

Letter to Editor:

At a meeting held last Friday evening, July 16, at New Hope Baptist Church, a group of American Negro citizens and parents of the children who have attended Lincoln Elementary Public School, voiced their sentiments concerning this school's existence in the following manner:

First—The already exisiting inadequacy of the over 100 year old building, the crowded condition and not sufficient teaching faculty for the number of children. Second—The hardship imposed on our children who must walk the distance from the East End and pass the Washington School to reach Lincoln. Third—We considered the destruction from the recent burning and do not expect to accept it repaired.

In a previous publication of this paper it was stated that we as a group were divided. We refute this statement as we may not all be able to express ourselves, but we are definitely together.

We are asking for integration of both pupils and teachers in the light of the Supreme Court decision and following the pattern of other Ohio cities, as we have some of the finest teachers in our group as ever graced any nation. If we do not have what is needed here it is available elsewhere and can be brought in. Since integration is what we want and we only have one teacher here with proper credentials we want her retained and placed along with our pupils, as there are two other buildings. This community has a right to look after its own constituents first and force public school education on all pupils alike. If there should be an influx of other American children to this area there would im can be afforded along with other Americans.

We cannot fight Communism with prejudice even though a statement made in the Cleveland Call Post of July 17, by our superintendent of schools that it did exist here.

Let us be fair m can citizens po of the Bib weapon of c and America cannot anytin defeated if we sure all minor a ed out. Jesus 15:33 "Greater l than this, that a n life for his friend. that we have made that contribution.

—Elder Rita E.
230 N. East St.,

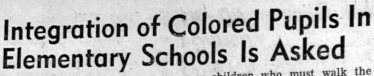

FOLLOW IN OUR FOOTSTEPS

Now you know what it was like to walk a mile (or six hundred miles!) in our shoes. It's up to you to carry the torch of justice. When you do, think of me, Joyce Clemons, my friends, and our mothers—the Lincoln School Marchers. Remember our fire for fairness and how we blazed a trail to equality.

And remember, there's a light inside you, too. **Let it shine!**

THE NINETEEN MOTHERS

Nellie
Zimmerman

Della
Blakey

alberta
Goins

Gertrude
Clemons

Roxie
Clemons

blea
Clemons

Zora-
Cumberland

Norma
Rollins

albert
Jewett

Minnie
Speach

Delia Cumberland

Imogene Curtis

Selicka Dent

ella Mae umberland

Maxine Thomas

Sallie Williams

Joanne Zimmerman

Elsie Steward Young

Frances Curtis

A NOTE FROM THE AUTHORS

The March
By taking all those steps every school day for two years, the mighty group of thirty-seven children and nineteen mothers made their town take a very important step toward equality.

The Lincoln School Marchers' movement started in 1954 and continued for two school years. That's longer than the thirteen-month Montgomery Bus Boycott of 1955! Each school day, the mothers and students marched a mile to school and after being turned away, walked back to the "Kitchen Schools" for their lessons. Over the course of those two years, the mothers and children walked more than six hundred miles in total. That's like walking from Hillsboro, Ohio to New York City!

In 1956, the federal court ruled that the Hillsboro School Board must integrate all of its schools. After the decision, Webster School finally admitted the Lincoln School Marchers. However, although the students had worked so hard and waited so long to attend Webster School, they were not all warmly welcomed or treated fairly as students there. Many of the Black children were held back two grades, even though they had attended school daily during the protest. Others were made to sit at the back of their class. Still, some children made friends and felt teachers were kind. We hope that this sad truth does not discourage you, the reader, from speaking up and taking action for a good cause.

Keeping Memories
Joyce Clemons did not really keep a memory book about her childhood experience as a Lincoln School Marcher. However, as an adult, Mrs. Joyce Clemons Kittrell and some of her marching friends—Myra Cumberland Phillips, Teresa Williams, Carolyn Steward Goins, Eleanor Curtis Cumberland, Virginia Steward Harewood, and Ralph Steward—decided that they wanted everyone to know their story. They wanted to honor the sacrifice their mothers made not only for them, but for all children. In the words of Eleanor Curtis Cumberland, ". . . that's my purpose—to see that my mama's work isn't lost. And that this fight goes on, that this story goes on" (qtd. in Rovan and Barnes 43).

Black Mothers Leading the Way
The mothers of Hillsboro were leaders and teachers who demanded equal rights, and the best education, for their children. The creators of this book are also Black mothers, and we are honored to share the story of this special group of women and children who have shown us the power of standing up and marching forward.

A NOTE FROM THE ILLUSTRATOR

I grew up going to majority white schools in Ohio. I often felt "other" as the only Black kid in my friend groups and felt especially alone when we covered Black History in Social Studies. I could feel my face turn hot when we talked about slavery! To imagine how these children felt at the time of the Lincoln School March challenges me to imagine things being incredibly tougher, and I am both grateful for them paving the way for future kids like me and in awe of the bravery of the mothers & fathers who marched for their babies. To be able to visually tell their story in partnership with Daydreamers Press and Ohio Humanities is an honor. This is for my glowing, growing Black boy, Damon Reggie, and for all my babies of the world who are smart, capable, brave and deserving of every opportunity afforded to their peers. I illustrate for you!

A NOTE FROM OHIO HUMANITIES

After *Brown v. Board of Education* was decided in 1954, a group of Black mothers in the small town of Hillsboro, Ohio, marched their children to the white school, demanding admission. After being rejected, they woke up the next morning and marched again. And again. And again. For two years, they marched. It took courage, determination, and strength to continue the fight, but they persisted. And they won.

Many of the Lincoln School students who marched are still alive today. As elementary school students, these brave individuals became activists, even if they didn't realize it at the time. *Step by Step* tells their story from the perspective of Joyce Clemons, one of the women who marched for integration as a child.

In sharing this story, Joyce and the other marchers hope to inspire others to remember their mothers and continue the work they started. Their commitment to keeping the story of the march—and their mothers—alive reminds us of the importance of education and of how recent the civil rights movement is in our past.

Ohio Humanities is proud to partner with Daydreamers Press to ensure that this story is not forgotten. By following in Joyce's footsteps, today's young readers will see how brave mothers and students just like them changed the course of history.

TIMELINE

May 1954 — *Brown v. Board of Education of Topeka* ruling is decided by the US Supreme Court, making segregation illegal in all public schools in the United States.

July 1954 — Phillip Patridge, a white man, breaks into Lincoln Elementary School, the only elementary school in Hillsboro, OH Black students attend, and sets it on fire as an attempt to integrate the schools.

August 1954 — A group of Black families attempt to enroll their children in Webster School, and the school board denies them.

September 1954 — A group of Black mothers arrive at Webster School with their children. The children are put on the roster and assigned rooms.

September 1954 — Schools close for two weeks for the Highland County Fair and the school board meets to rezone the district, keeping the Black students enrolled at Lincoln.

September 1954 — Nineteen mothers and thirty-seven children meet each weekday to march to Webster School in protest.

September 1954 — Five mothers (Gertrude Clemons, Roxie Clemons, Elsie Steward, Norma Rollins, Zella Mae Cumberland) file a lawsuit with Joyce Clemons, daughter of Gertrude, as the lead plaintiff.

September 1955 — The march to Webster School continues for a second school year.

April 1956 — The court rules that the Hillsboro School Board must integrate all schools.

April 1956 — The Lincoln School Marchers attend their first day at Webster School.

2015 — The Lincoln School Marchers, now adults, begin to share their story.

THE LINCOLN SCHOOL STUDENT MARCHERS

(L-R) Virginia Steward Hareword, Teresa Williams, Joyce Clemons Kittrell, Carolyn Steward Goins, Eleanor Curtis Cumberland, Myra Cumberland Phillips.
Photo courtesy of Ohio Humanities.

MARCHERS, CONTINUED

John Cumberland, Jr.
Myra Cumberland Phillips
Doris Cumberland Woods
John Curtis
Lawrence Curtis
Lee Curtis
Marva Curtis
Dorothy Clemons Ford
Joyce Clemons Kittrell
Sarah Alice Clemons
Rosemary Clemons Cumberland
Billy Dent
Glen Dent
Lynn Dent
Glenna Dent Hennison
Rev. Michael Hudson
Lewis Goins
David Butch Johnson

Charles Johnson
Annabell Johnson Smith
Debbie Rollins
Evelyn Steward Bostie
Ralph Steward
Carolyn Steward Goins
Virginia Steward Harewood
Jean Speach Williams
Brenda Thomas Coleman
Delbert Thomas
Harold Joe Thomas
Winnie Thomas Cumberland
Howard Williams
Peggy Williams Hudson
Mary Williams Steward
Teresa Williams
Diane Zimmerman Curtis

QUOTATIONS IN THE STORY

Most of the quotations in the story are real—based on oral history, news reports, and other primary sources. One important quote the authors created for the story is, "According to the law of the USA, Hillsboro cannot keep Black children in separate, unequal schools." We wrote this quote based on the beliefs we know that Mrs. Imogene Curtis and the other mothers held.

SPECIAL THANKS

Dear Lincoln School Alumni of Hillsboro, Ohio,
You resolved to record your story into history for the next generations of children and to honor your mothers on the record. Thank you for sharing your lives with us and trusting us to tell your story. We hope we have made you and your mothers proud.

Thank you to all of the Marching Mothers and children, to their fathers and families, and to the community who supported this movement. Special thanks to Ohio Humanities and the Highland County Historical Society for helping to record and amplify this important history.

BIBLIOGRAPHY

Burwinkel, Kati, et al. *Black History of Highland County Ohio*. 2nd ed., 2022.

Meier, August and Elliott Rudwick. "Early Boycotts of Segregated Schools: The Case of

Springfield, Ohio, 1922-23." *American Quarterly*, Vol. 20, no. 4, 1968, pp. 744-58.

Rogers, Alexis. "Meet the Hillsboro Marching Mothers who helped change the course of

history." *WLWT5*, 6 March 2017,

https://www.wlwt.com/amp/article/meet-the-hillsboro-marching-mothers-who-

helped-change-the-course-of-history/8981617.

Rovan, Aaron, and Melvin Barnes. "Marching On." *Lumen Magazine*, vol. I, 2023,

pp. 26-49.

https://www.ohiohumanities.org/wp-content/uploads/2022/08/LUMEN-

LincolnSchoolMarchers-FINAL.pdf.

Torrice, Andrea, director. *The Lincoln School Story: The Battle for School Integration* in

Ohio. 2022. *Ohio Humanities*,

https://www.ohiohumanities.org/lincoln-school-marchers-documentary/.

IMAGES

4, background: *The News-Herald*. 4, lower left: *Jet*/J. Paul Getty Trust and Smithsonian National Museum of African American History and Culture. 5, center: *Hillsboro Press-Gazette*. 5, upper right: Highland County Historical Society, Lincoln School Collection. 9, upper right: *Hillsboro Press-Gazette*. 9, lower left: *The News-Herald*. 12, upper: Highland County Historical Society, Lincoln School Collection. 12, lower left: Getty Images. 12, lower right: Highland County Historical Society, Lincoln School Collection. 14: Getty Images. 16, upper: Cleveland State University. 16, center: *Jet*/J. Paul Getty Trust and Smithsonian National Museum of African American History and Culture. 16, lower: *Cincinnati Post*. 20: *Cleveland Call and Post*. 24: *Hillsboro Press-Gazette*. 27, lower left: *Hillsboro Press-Gazette*. 32, upper: *Hillsboro Press-Gazette*. 32, center: Getty Images. 32, lower left: *Cincinnati Post*. 32, lower right corner: Highland County Historical Society. Back cover: *Cincinnati Post*. Additional images courtesy of Eleanor Curtis Cumberland, Joyce Clemons Kittrell, Myra Cumberland Phillips, and Shellee Fischer.

ABOUT THE AUTHORS

Step by step, Debbie Rigaud has written several middle grade and young adult books and is the co-author of the *New York Times* bestseller *The Sister Switch* and the Hope series. Her next picture book is *The Littlest Food Critic*. Debbie grew up in East Orange, NJ, and lives with her husband and children in Columbus, OH. Visit her at www.debbierigaud.com.

Carlotta Penn has loved writing since she was a young girl. At age eight she wrote in her diary, "I love to write books. I am an author." Now all grown up, she has written several picture books, including *Bright Boy ABCs* and the The Turtle With an Afro series. She plans to write many more. Carlotta lives in Columbus, OH, with her husband and three children.

DEDICATION

Dear Black Mothers, thank you for loving and leading us all.
—CMP, DR

THIS PROJECT IS SUPPORTED IN PART BY OHIO HUMANITIES' GENEROUS CONVERSATION STARTERS:

John M. Glaze in honor of the Lincoln School Marchers

Arthur and Kathleen Bauer
David Descutner and DeLysa Burnier in honor of Ada Woodson Adams and Dr. Francine Childs
Kristy Eckert Communications in honor of Kim Eckert and Shelley Rogers
Dr. Rustom and Mary Khouri in honor of Susan F. Smith
Doreen Uhas Sauer and John Sauer in memory of Cathy D. Nelson (1951—2022)
Susan F. Smith and Bob Smith in honor of Mary Jane Ferraro, Mary Margaret Smith, and Carmella Mazzella Ferraro

Rebecca Brown Asmo in honor of Marisa Brown
Anne and Tim Bezbatchenko in honor of Jack and Sarah Bezbatchenko
Douglas and Marisa Brown in memory of Beryl Force and Faustina Cenci
Katherine Fell in honor of Winzer and Vivian Andrews
Shellee Fisher in honor of Marqus, Jr. and Camille Crawford
Catherine and Steve Kennedy in honor of Seyla Kramer
Dan Moder in memory of Susan E. Chenault
Mary Jane and Jim Pajk in honor of Janice Pajk and Shirley McLean
Frances Penn in memory of Gary M. Penn, Sr.
Diana, Chris, and Scarlett Rebman in memory of Delores "Dee" Rebman
Sarah Sisser in honor of Barb Lockard
Amy Grace and Doug Ulman in honor of Diana Ulman and Johanna Roussel

Kathy Sue Barker
Judith and Richard Bryan
Brodi and Andrea Conover
Deena Epstein
Ivy Freeman
John and Carolyn Kellis

Vicki Knauff
Philip Kuceyeski
Kevin and Carla Miller
Heather and Gary Ness
Carey Schmitt
Paul Watkins

Published by Daydreamers Press
daydreamerspress.com

Inquiries welcomed at daydreamerspress@gmail.com.

Ohio Humanities is the state-based partner of the National Endowment for the Humanities. Any views, findings, conclusions or recommendations expressed in publication do not necessarily represent those of the National Endowment for the Humanities.

For more on the Ohio Humanities Lincoln School Marchers project visit
www.ohiohumanities.org/lincoln-school/

ohc@ohiohumanities.org

Manufactured in the United States of America

978-0-9996613-8-3

Printed in the USA
CPSIA information can be obtained
at www.ICGtesting.com
JSRC081744261123
52338JS00007B/23